*The American Economy,
1960–2000: A Retrospective and
Prospective Look*

THE CHARLES C. MOSKOWITZ MEMORIAL
LECTURES

NUMBER XXIII

Richard M. Cyert

President
Carnegie-Mellon University

Discussants
Henry C. Lucas, Jr.

Professor of Computer Applications and Information Systems,
Chairman, Department of Computer Application and Information Systems,
New York University

William Silber

Professor of Economics and Finance
New York University

The American Economy, 1960–2000:
A Retrospective and Prospective Look

The Charles C. Moskowitz Memorial Lectures,
College of Business and Public Administration
New York University

THE FREE PRESS
A Division of Macmillan Publishing Co., Inc.
NEW YORK

Collier Macmillan Publishers
LONDON

Copyright © 1983 by New York University

All rights reserved. No part of this book may be reproduced or transmitted in any form or by any means, electronic or mechanical, including photocopying, recording, or by any information storage and retrieval system, without permission in writing from the Publisher.

The Free Press
A Division of Macmillan Publishing Co., Inc.
866 Third Avenue, New York, N.Y. 10022

Collier Macmillan Canada, Inc.

Library of Congress Cataloging in Publication Data

Cyert, Richard Michael
  The American economy, 1960–2000.

  (The Charles C. Moskowitz memorial lectures; no. 23)
  1. United States—Economic conditions—1961–1971.
  2. United States—Economic conditions—1971–
  3. Economic forecasting—United States. I. Lucas, Henry C. II. Silber, William L. III. Title.
  IV. Series.
  HC106.6.C9   1982   330.973′092   82-48600
  ISBN 0-02-923100-0

Printed in the United States of America

printing number
1 2 3 4 5 6 7 8 9 10

FOREWORD

This volume, the twenty–third in the Charles C. Moskowitz Memorial lecture series (see p. 15), is concerned with the state of the American economy, taking a retrospective look backward to 1960 and a prospective look forward to 2000. It seemed especially appropriate to do at this time, partly because of current concern over the economy and partly because this is the sesquicentennial year of New York University's existence.

It is a simple observation of reality that the American economy which for generations was regarded as an economic marvel of creativity and productivity, is no longer regarded with such high esteem and respect. Where a bare dozen or so years ago Jean-Jacques Servan-Schrieber in France warned western Europe that the American economic juggernaut was in the process of achieving dominance, today both western Europeans and Americans look with a mixture of awe and envy at the competitive triumphs of Japanese industry. And it has become the popular wisdom of the day to bemoan the decline of productivity, creativity, and the work ethic in America. We got caught up in the myth of our mastery of production, and we acted as though our fundamental and long-range problems related essentially to distribution and consumption. Now we appear to be relearning a fundamental fact; namely, consumption requires production, just as, in a market economy, production requires effective demand.

We were fortunate to have Dr. Richard M. Cyert, a distinguished economist and president of Carnegie–Mellon University, as our lecturer. Born and reared in Minnesota, he earned his baccalaureate degree at that state's great university, following which he came to Columbia University for his Ph.D. A brilliant scholar and educator, he distinguished himself as an academic administrator and director of major corporations.

We were fortunate also to have as discussants two distinguished scholars, both of them from New York University's Faculty of Business Administration. Dr. Henry C. Lucas, Jr., professor and chairman of the Department of Computer Applications and Information Systems, and Dr. William Silber, professor of economics and finance, added incisive insights in their comments on Dr. Cyert's lecture.

I express appreciation to Susan Landis and Virginia Moress for handling all the arrangements for the lectures, and also to Professors Jules Backman, Ernest Bloch, and Ernest Kurnow, who comprise the faculty members of the Charles C. Moskowitz Memorial Lectures Committee.

Finally, I express appreciation for the efficiency and care with which The Free Press handled the production of this volume.

It would not be an excusable oversight if I failed to note now Professor Backman's untimely and sudden death a few days prior to this lecture. He played a prominent role in bringing the lecture series to its present position of substantive significance, and that role should be recognized explicitly and publicly. In fact, his role at New York University, for over half a century, was so outstanding that I believe it appropriate to include in this foreword my remarks on the occasion of the services in his memory.

My mind is filled with memories. My eyes are filled with tears. A great and good man has slipped away from us, and gone to eternity. But after our tears have dried, our memories will remain. And they will continually enrich our lives, for they will remind us of Jules and his extraordinary achievements.
Jules was a master teacher.
Jules was a superb scholar.
Jules was a great humanitarian.
Jules was dedicated to excellence.
He was not given to softly-worded distortions of the truth, and for this generations of students and young colleagues will be forever in his debt. My association with him goes back 35 years, to the day I arrived as a young instructor at the School of Commerce. I was among those who were privileged to work with him on articles as well as national wage cases. He showed the way to the refereed learned journals. He lighted the path along which one could progress in one's career. He taught us and guided us, and, without him, we would have been less than we became. Some of us even began to wear bow ties.
Jules' knowledge of economics was extraordinary; his grasp of data and the methodology behind its

compilation was startling. But more important was his conceptual mastery. He understood the system and its myriad and complex interrelationships. And he had the marvelous ability to make it clear and comprehensible to others. His published works are almost beyond count. In fact, I will confess that I have for years, played a little game; the object of which was to find a significant library somewhere that did not have one or more of Jules' publications in its collections. Nowhere have I been successful in locating such a library.

Jules' concern for his fellow men was noble. In its purity of purpose, its constructiveness and achievement of results. He did not simply talk; he did. He loved Hebrew Union College. He loved New York University. And this magnificent building, as well as the Jules Backman Amphitheatre in Tisch Hall and the Jules Backman Faculty Fellowships in Business Economics at the Graduate School of Business Administration symbolize the depth and the extent of that love.

For his sterling character and myriad good works he received such honors as we could bestow. But I know in my heart that what he treasured most, what he valued highest, was the deep love they reflected and symbolized.

Teacher, scholar, humanitarian; much indeed. But not all that was Jules is captured by those words. To comprehend him whole, one must recognize his devotion to his family. As the years passed and the nature of our relationship deepened and became more personal, I came to appreciate that devotion. I observed the love he had for Grace, for John, for Susan, and for his grandchildren. One had to be deeply moved, and I was.

Oh Lord—how we will miss him.

April 12, 1982

Abraham L. Gitlow, Dean
College of Business and
   Public Administration
New York University

THE CHARLES C. MOSKOWITZ MEMORIAL LECTURES

THE CHARLES C. MOSKOWITZ MEMORIAL LECTURES were established through the generosity of a distinguished alumnus of the College of Business and Public Administration, the late Charles C. Moskowitz of the Class of 1914.

It was Mr. Moskowitz's aim to contribute to the understanding of functional issues of major concern to business and the nation by providing a public forum for the dissemination of enlightened business theories and practices.

A pioneer in the American motion-picture industry, Charles Moskowitz worked with other innovators to create a business and entertainment phenomenon of enormous influence. He retired only after many years as Vice-President and Treasurer, and a Director, of Loew's, Inc.

This volume is the twenty-third in the Moskowitz series. The earlier ones are:

February, 1961   *Business Survival in the Sixties*
Thomas F. Patton, President and Chief Executive Officer
Republic Steel Corporation

November, 1961   *The Challenges Facing Management*
Don G. Mitchell, President
General Telephone and Electronics Corporation

November, 1962   *Competitive Private Enterprise Under Government Regulation*
Malcolm A. MacIntyre, President
Eastern Air Lines

November, 1963   *The Common Market: Friend or Competitor?*
Jesse W. Markham, Professor of Economics, Princeton University
Charles E. Fiero, Vice President, The Chase Manhattan Bank
Howard S. Piquet, Senior Specialist in International Economics, Legislative Reference Service, The Library of Congress

November, 1964   *The Forces Influencing the American Economy*
Jules Backman, Research Professor of Economics, New York University
Martin R. Gainsbrugh, Chief Economist and Vice President, National Industrial Conference Board

November, 1965   *The American Market of the Future*
                             Arno H. Johnson, Vice President and Senior Economist, J. Walter Thompson Company
                             Gilbert E. Jones, President, IBM World Trade Corporation
                             Darrell B. Lucas, Professor of Marketing and Chairman of the Department, New York University

November, 1966   *Government Wage-Price Guideposts in the American Economy*
                             George Meany, President, American Federation of Labor and Congress of Industrial Organizations
                             Roger M. Blough, Chairman of the Board and Chief Executive Officer, United States Steel Corporation
                             Neil H. Jacoby, Dean, Graduate School of Business Administration, University of California at Los Angeles

November, 1967   *The Defense Sector in the American Economy*
                             Jacob K. Javits, United States Senator, New York
                             Charles J. Hitch, President, University of California
                             Arthur F. Burns, Chairman, Federal Reserve Board

November, 1968   *The Urban Environment: How It Can Be Improved*

William E. Zisch, Vice-chairman of the Board, Aerojet-General Corporation
Paul H. Douglas, Chairman, National Commission on Urban Problems
Professor of Economics, New School for Social Research
Robert C. Weaver, President, Bernard M. Baruch College of the City University of New York
Former Secretary of Housing and Urban Development

November, 1969 *Inflation: The Problem It Creates and the Policies It Requires*
Arthur M. Okun, Senior Fellow, The Brookings Institution
Henry H. Fowler, General Partner, Goldman, Sachs & Co.
Milton Gilbert, Economic Adviser, Bank for International Settlements

March, 1971 *The Economics of Pollution*
Kenneth E. Boulding, Professor of Economics, University of Colorado
Elvis J. Stahr, President, National Audubon Society
Solomon Fabricant, Professor of Economics New York University
Former Director, National Bureau of Economic Research
Martin R. Gainsbrugh, Adjunct Professor of Economics, New York University

Chief Economist, National Industrial Conference Board

April, 1971
Young America in the NOW World
Hubert H. Humphrey, Senator from Minnesota
Former Vice President of the United States

April, 1972
Optimum Social Welfare and Productivity: A Comparative View
Jan Tinbergen, Professor of Development Planning, Netherlands School of Economics
Abram Bergson, George E. Baker Professor of Economics, Harvard University
Fritz Machlup, Professor of Economics, New York University
Oskar Morgenstern, Professor of Economics, New York University

April, 1973
Fiscal Responsibility: Tax Increases or Spending Cuts?
Paul McCracken, Edmund Ezra Day University, Professor of Business Administration, University of Michigan
Murray L. Weidenbaum, Edward Mallinckrodt Distinguished University Professor, Washington University
Lawrence S. Ritter, Professor of Finance, New York University
Robert A. Kavesh, Professor of Finance, New York University

March 1974   *Wall Street in Transition: The Emerging System and its Impact on the Economy*
Henry G. Manne, Distinguished Professor of Law, Director of the Center for Studies in Law and Economics, University of Miami Law School
Ezra Solomon, Dean Witter Professor of Finance, Stanford University

March, 1975   *Leaders and Followers in an Age of Ambiguity*
George P. Shultz, Professor, Graduate School of Business, Stanford University
President, Bechtel Corporation

March, 1976   *The Economic System in an Age of Discontinuity: Long-Range Planning or Market Reliance?*
Wassily Leontief, Nobel Laureate Professor of Economics, New York University
Herbert Stein, A. Willis Robertson Professor of Economics, University of Virginia

March, 1977   *Demographic Dynamics in America*
Wilber J. Cohen, Dean of the School of Education and Professor of Education and of Public Welfare Administration University of Michigan
Charles F. Westoff, Director of the Office of Population Research and

Maurice During Professor of Demographic Studies, Princeton University

March, 1978 *The Rediscovery of the Business Cycle*
Paul A. Volcker, President and Chief Executive Officer, Federal Reserve Bank of New York

March, 1979 *Economic Pressure and the Future of The Arts*
William Schuman, Composer
Roger L. Stevens, Chairman of the Board of Trustees, John F. Kennedy Center for the Performing Arts

April, 1980 *Presidential Promises and Performance*
McGeorge Bundy, Professor of History, Faculty of Arts and Science, New York University
Edmund S. Muskie, Former U.S. Senator from Minnesota, Secretary of State

April, 1981 *Econometric Models as Guides for Decision Making*
Lawrence R. Klein, Benjamin Franklin Professor of Finance and Economics, University of Pennsylvania

Note: All but the last five volumes of The Charles C. Moskowitz Memorial Lectures were published by New York University Press, 21 West Fourth Street, New York, N.Y. 10003. The 1977, 1978, 1979, 1980, and 1981 lectures were published by The Free Press.

CONTENTS

FOREWORD 5
    Abraham L. Gitlow

THE AMERICAN ECONOMY, 1960–2000:
A RETROSPECTIVE AND PROSPECTIVE LOOK
                                                25
    Richard M. Cyert

DISCUSSANTS
    Henry C. Lucas, Jr.   71
    William L. Silber   81

THE AMERICAN ECONOMY, 1960-2000: A RETROSPECTIVE AND PROSPECTIVE LOOK

Richard M. Cyert
President
Carnegie–Mellon University

The year 2000 which has held a magical quality is looming on the horizon, so it seems a good time to take stock of the economy. Where have we been and where are we going? In this lecture, I look at the performance of the economy over the past twenty years and attempt to assess our future, at least to the year 2000.

Meaning of Performance

This talk will be organized around the four main functions that an economy must perform.[1] First the public must decide *what goods and services will be produced*. There must be mechanisms within the system to decide the range of goods and services that will be produced and in what quantities. This function includes the division between the government and the private sector with respect to the resources that each will control.

Second, the public must determine *how its goods and services will be produced*. In particular, the system must determine the amount of capital and labor that goes into the act of production. We will try to detect how the labor force is changing and the areas in which it is working. We are also concerned with determining how our methods of production compare with competitors from other countries.

Third, the public must determine *who will get the goods and services produced*. We will be concerned with the questions of how well our economy performs its basic function of improving the quality of life for our population.

Finally, the public must decide *how much of its economic resources to devote to future growth and how much to satisfy current consumption desires*. We will be interested in particular in the question of investment in plant and equipment.

These are the basic functions of an economy, but in evaluating performance we must also be interested in such questions as the stability of the performance. In our economy, we are concerned with the question of the business cycle. We need to look at the various macroeconomic policies that have been followed over the past twenty years. We need also to examine the serious problems of unemployment and inflation that have plagued the economy and the sick industries that exist currently.

Mix of Goods and Services Produced

One way of understanding the complex of goods and services produced is to examine the proportion of the Gross National Product (GNP) produced by each sector. Table 1 shows such a distribution and also shows the relative stability of the sectors. Part of the reason for the stability is the tremendous aggregation involved in the allocation of GNP to a small number

Table 1. GNP Distribution by Sector

	Agriculture	Mining	Construction	Manufacturing	Transportation & Public Utilities	Trade (Wholesale & Retail)	Services (Finance & Other)	Government
1960	4.4%	2.0%	6.2%	23.4%	7.9%	16.0%	25.1%	14.6%
1979	3.3%	2.9%	4.8%	24.0%	8.9%	16.6%	27.6%	11.8%

Source: 1979 Business Statistics.
July 1981, Supplement to *Survey of Current Business*.

Table 2. Labor Distribution by Sector

	Agriculture	Mining	Construction	Manufacturing	Transportation & Public Utilities	Trade (Wholesale & Retail)	Services (Finance & Other)	Government
1960	8.7%	1.0%	5.0%	24.6%	6.0%	20.8%	18.9%	15.0%
1979	4.2%	1.1%	5.9%	22.3%	5.6%	20.5%	24.1%	16.3%

Source: 1979 Business Statistics.
July 1981, Supplement to *Survey of Current Business*.

of categories. In addition, however, the stability represents the fact that the United States is a mature society. The decline in the government sector is, perhaps, surprising, but it must be remembered that transfer payments are not included and there has been a large growth of such payments. The other changes of interest are in agriculture and construction. Each area is producing a smaller percentage of the GNP than in 1960.

Table 2 is somewhat more interesting than Table 1. We see the way in which labor is distributed by sector. There are two rather startling results. The percentage of the labor force in agriculture has declined by 4.5 percentage points. On a percentage basis this is a decline of more than 50 percent between 1960 and 1979. Since the labor force had increased less than that in the period under consideration, we can conclude that there are fewer people working in agriculture than in 1960. The service sector also shows significant results with an increase 5.2 percentage points, an increase of 27.5 percent in the proportion of the labor force in the service sector. Two other changes of interest are in manufacturing and government. Manufacturing's share of the labor force has decreased 2.3 percentage points and government's has gone up by 1.3 percentage points. Interestingly, the decreases in agriculture and manufacturing are about equal to the increases in services and government, 6.8 versus 6.5. In other words, it is as though about 6.5 percent of the 1979 labor force shifted out of agriculture or manufacturing and moved to the service sector or government sometime over the period from 1960 to 1979.

Overall, one must conclude that the economy's

decision makers are deciding that about the same goods and services should be produced today as in the past, although there is evidence that some changes are occurring. In particular, there is a shift of the labor force into the service and government areas. The movement is partly in response to the demands of the public since they influence the price system which in turn determines the way resources in the private sector are allocated in our economy. The figures probably mask the greater demands of government as a result of increased and more complex regulations. For example, the declines in the percentage of the labor force in manufacturing and agriculture are probably smaller than would have been realized if regulations had not been so extensive.

Production of Goods and Services

The basic question in examining the way in which goods and services are produced relates to the productivity of the factors of production. The structure of our economy is a competitive one. We pride ourselves on producing in the most efficient manner possible. If a firm does not follow the most efficient techniques then in our system that firm will be driven out of business. For our purposes it will be informative to look first at changes in the amount of capital per worker in our system. We are interested in examining the changes in productivity and one of the critical variables is the amount of capital in the system.

Table 3 gives the values of an index of capital per worker based on 1972. The index number is given for each of the three sectors that embrace the entire

Table 3. Capital Per Worker*

	Farm	Manufacturing	Nonfarm Nonmanufacturing
1960	51.1	76.6	71.2
1961	53.3	77.5	74.3
1962	55.2	77.0	76.7
1963	59.5	77.8	79.0
1964	64.4	79.2	81.1
1965	68.9	79.2	83.6
1966	77.3	79.8	86.1
1967	82.1	84.5	87.5
1968	83.0	86.6	89.9
1969	89.2	88.2	92.5
1970	94.2	94.9	96.3
1971	97.7	100.3	103.1
1972	100.0	100.0	100.0
1973	101.7	97.5	101.9
1974	107.7	102.7	104.1
1975	110.8	116.1	108.0
1976	109.5	114.6	106.0
1977	119.4	114.8	103.8
1978	119.9	114.4	101.5
1979	125.8	116.6	100.7
1972 =	$18,245/worker	$11,125/worker	$14,960/worker

*Workers calculated by converting part-time and sole proprietor hours into full-time workers by dividing by part-time hours per full-time employee in each sector. Capital is constant dollar net stock of private non-residential capital.
Source: Capital Stock data from February 1981, *Survey of Current Business*.
   Labor data 1960–1974 from *The National Income and Product Accounts 1929–1974*.
   1975 from July 1976 *Survey of Current Business*
   1976–1979 from July 1981 *Survey of Current Business*.

economy. Clearly agriculture has made the greatest progress since 1960 and the nonfarm, nonmanufacturing sector has made the least in increasing the amount of capital available for each full-time worker. This fact is of particular interest since, as we have seen from Table 2, more of the labor force has been shifting into that sector from agriculture and man-

Table 4. Capital Per Workers' Annual Growth Rates*

	Farm	Manufacturing	Nonfarm Nonmanufacturing
1960–1970	6.31%	2.17%	3.07%
1970–1979	3.27%	2.31%	0.50%

*Capital is constant dollar net stock of private nonresidential structures and equipment. Workers calculated by converting part-time and self-employed hours into full-time equivalents using hours per full-time employee for each sector.

Source: Capital Data from *Survey of Current Business*, February, 1981.
  1960 and 1970 Data from *The National Income and Product Accounts 1929–1974*.
  1979 Labor Data from *Survey of Current Business*, July 1981.

ufacturing. Table 4 gives some additional insight into the problem. The annual growth rates broken into decades show a significant drop in the 1970s in agriculture and in the nonfarm, nonmanufacturing sector. Manufacturing has maintained a low, but steady growth during the twenty years.

Table 5 shows in some detail the annual rates of productivity by sectors of the economy. The overall impact of the table is the striking increase in negative signs in the 1970s. Table 6 gives summary measures of the two decades by showing the annual compound rates of growth. It is clear from this chart that productivity growth in the 1970s was clearly reduced from the 1960s.

The measurement of productivity is not an easy matter. The rates of growth in Table 5 have been calculated in the usual way which is to relate gross domestic product and hours worked by each sector. Regardless of the precision of the measure it is clear that general trends appear that are exceedingly discouraging for the United States.

Table 5. Annual Rates of Productivity Increases

	Total Nonfarm	Agriculture	Mining	Construction	Manufacturing	Transportation & Public Utilities	Trade (Wholesale & Retail)	Services (Finance & Other)	Government
1960	1.0%	—	—	—	—	—	—	—	—
1961	2.6%	4.7%	4.7%	1.6%	2.2%	4.3%	2.8%	2.3%	0.3%
1962	4.3%	4.1%	5.3%	0.9%	4.2%	4.6%	5.7%	3.2%	2.0%
1963	3.5%	2.3%	5.8%	0.2%	7.0%	5.4%	3.6%	-0.8%	-0.7%
1964	3.6%	5.4%	2.7%	4.9%	5.2%	3.4%	7.5%	1.2%	0.8%
1965	3.3%	6.1%	1.8%	1.6%	3.6%	5.5%	3.7%	2.5%	1.1%
1966	2.6%	3.9%	4.8%	1.2%	1.3%	4.5%	3.7%	0.6%	-0.9%
1967	1.6%	8.6%	4.6%	1.2%	0.3%	1.7%	2.2%	0.9%	0.9%
1968	3.2%	-0.2%	4.1%	3.0%	4.4%	5.4%	4.5%	1.7%	0.4%
1969	-0.3%	5.6%	0.6%	-7.8%	1.3%	-0.5%	0.8%	0.8%	0.8%

1970	0.1%	7.7%	2.2%	−4.2%	0.8%	1.9%	1.1%	2.3%	1.0%
1971	3.1%	6.0%	0.4%	2.1%	5.7%	3.4%	2.8%	1.7%	1.4%
1972	3.7%	−2.3%	−3.2%	−2.3%	−2.3%	5.2%	5.6%	1.6%	1.4%
1973	1.7%	2.4%	−0.7%	−6.2%	9.0%	4.9%	3.1%	0.7%	0.4%
1974	−3.1%	−4.2%	−8.2%	−5.5%	−4.0%	−1.8%	−3.4%	−0.2%	−0.2%
1975	1.8%	10.4%	−9.3%	4.2%	1.9%	5.7%	3.0%	−0.2%	0.2%
1976	3.5%	−4.9%	−2.6%	3.4%	12.9%	6.9%	2.0%	5.2%	1.6%
1977	1.6%	4.9%	−2.8%	−2.1%	2.6%	2.4%	1.4%	1.2%	0.4%
1978	0.5%	−0.8%	−2.7%	−5.1%	0.8%	1.9%	1.0%	0.7%	0.2%
1979	−1.1%	5.7%	−5.6%	−6.7%	0.9%	0.5%	0.0%	−0.7%	0.6%

Source: Based on gross produce by sector and hours worked per sector.
Data 1975 from July 1976, *Survey of Current Business*.
Data 1976–1979 from July 1981, *Survey of Current Business*.
Data 1960–1974 from *National Income and Product Accounts 1929–1974*.

Table 6. Productivity Rates of Increase

	Agriculture	Mining	Construction	Manufacturing	Transportation & Public Utilities	Trade (Wholesale & Retail)	Services (Finance & Other)	Government
1960–1970	4.40%	3.64%	0.20%	2.98%	3.90%	3.05%	1.45%	0.48%
1970–1979	1.74%	−3.60%	−2.66%	2.92%	3.19%	1.69%	1.10%	0.63%

Source: Based on gross produce by sector and hours worked per sector.
Data 1975 from July 1976, *Survey of Current Business*.
Data 1976–1979 from July 1981, *Survey of Current Business*.
Data 1960–1974 from *National Income and Product Accounts 1929–1974*.

Because our knowledge on productivity is inexact, almost everyone concerned with the problem has advanced one or more reasons to explain the perverse trends. Edward Dennison has analyzed productivity with a view toward determining the variables and allocating the percentage points that each variable contributed to the growth rate. His determinants of output seem to account for the drop in productivity rates until 1974. The contributions of his catchall variable, "advances in knowledge and miscellaneous determinants" to explaining the productivity rate fell from 1.4 percent in 1978 to −0.8 percent a year in the 1973–1976 period. In attempting to explain this drop, he states, "Seventeen suggested reasons for the slowdown in my residual series were explored in this chapter. I rejected a few suggestions, expressed skepticism about some, had no opinion about others and characterized the rest as probably correct but individually able to explain only a small part of the slowdown. No single hypothesis seems to provide a probable explanation of the sharp change after 1973."[2]

The reasons Dennison explores run the gamut of "reasonable explanations." The answer as he suggests is probably the result of a large number of reasons each of which has contributed only a few tenths of a percentage to the total explanation. In the evaluation of the performance of the economy, it is clear that the drop in productivity has been a major adverse factor on living standards. In addition, it increases conflicts over income distribution because such conflicts become greater when the total to be divided is not growing adequately. Concern over distribution leads us to the next measure of performance.

Distribution of Goods and Services

No measure of performance is complete without knowing the ultimate distribution of goods and services. Clearly this distribution depends on the way income is distributed. In the United States it is necessary to distinguish the income distribution before and after taxes and transfer payments. It is also necessary to take into account other benefits from government expenditures. In general it can be said that the effect of the tax system and the transfer payments is to make the income distribution after taxes less unequal than before. The net result of the combination of the functioning of the economic system, the tax system, the in-kind benefits and the transfer payments has been to improve the economic conditions of an increasing number of people. One measure justifying this assertion is the reduced number of people below the poverty level as shown in Table 7. If in-kind transfers are included that percentage of persons below the poverty line would go down even further. We are looking only at short-run effects on distribution and not making any effort to judge the long-run effect of a system

Table 7. Persons Below Poverty Line

	1960	1965	1975	1980
Number of persons (in thousands)	39,851	33,185	25,877	29,272
Percentage of population	22.2%	17.3%	12.3%	13.0%

Based on money income only—Includes Cash Welfare
—Excludes Food Stamps, Medicaid
Note: Increase 1979–1980 due to inflation's impact on Nominal Poverty Line.
Source: *Bureau of Census Current Population Reports, Series P-60 #127,* August 1981.

of taxes and transfer payments that achieves the results shown.

Another measure of interest is the per capita personal income. Table 8, shows the data for 1960, 1970, and 1980. The results are given in 1972 dollars and show a healthy rate of increase for both decades. In comparison, for example, the rate of increase in per capita income from 1950 to 1960 was only 1.23 percent but was between 2 and 3 percent over the two decades being analyzed. The median income from 1960 to 1970 increased at a rate of 2.95 percent, but from 1970 to 1980 the rate of increase in the median income was a miniscule 0.03 percent. The decade of the 1970s did not show significant improvement in the size of the median income. The index for real average hourly compensation for workers in the nonfarm business, for example, went down from 104.7 percent in 1970 to 99.4 percent in 1979 where 1977 is the

Table 8. Income Measures

	1960	1970	1980
Per Capita Disposal Personal Income (1972 dollars)[a]	$2,697	$ 3,619	$ 4,474
Compound Rate of Increase for previous decade		2.98%	2.14%
Median Income (1972 dollars)		$7,949[b]	$10,633[b] $10,699[c]
Compound Rate of Increase for previous period		2.95%	0.03%

Source: [a]*Handbook of Cyclical Indicators*, May 1977, U.S. Department of Commerce and *Business Condition Digest*, U.S. Department of Commerce, August 1981.
    [b]Current Population Reports, Series P-60, #129, U.S. Department of Commerce.
    [c]Current Population Reports, Series P-60, #127, U.S. Department of Commerce. (Put in 1972 dollars by use of Consumer Price Index by author.)

base year. This lack of growth in median income is a strong negative element in the performance of the economy for the 1970s.

The data does not show significant changes in the distribution of income. Table 9 indicates that the distribution of income in the population has remained relatively constant. One can also see from this data a result consistent with the data on the median income in Table 8. If we assume that income is uniformly distributed in the third fifth, that is, a given percent of the people in that category get that same percentage of income, then we see that in 1960 50 percent of the income recipients received 22.6 percent of the income. In 1970, the percentage was 22.5 percent, but in 1979 it was 21.7 percent. This change is consistent with the relatively small increase in the median income from 1970 to 1979.

There is, perhaps, a slight trend toward income becoming less equally distributed. Yet if we go back to the 1923–1929 period we see that the top 5 percent of people had 25.2 percent of the income. The 1979 data shows a significant decrease to 17.4 percent, for

Table 9. Percentage Distribution of Aggregate Income

	Lowest Fifth	Second Fifth	Third Fifth	Fourth Fifth	Highest Fifth	Top 5%
1960	3.2%	10.6%	17.6%	24.7%	44.0%	17.0%
1970	3.6%	10.3%	17.2%	24.7%	44.1%	16.9%
1979	3.8%	9.7%	16.4%	24.8%	45.3%	17.4%
1923–1929						25.2%
1946–1948						17.6%

Source: U.S. Department of Commerce, *Current Population Reports*, Series P-60 #129.
The Economic Order, Paul T. Homan, et al., p. 319.

the top 5 percent of income recipients. On balance then it seems from this data that we were better off, in 1980 than in 1950, but that most of the gain occurred in the 1960s. The 1970s have proved to be a relatively poor period for improving the economic fortunes of the population. The only way in which a country can improve the position of its population in real terms is by increasing productivity and increasing it relatively more than the population increases. Productivity growth as we have seen has significantly slowed in the United States in recent years and has even been negative in some periods. The result in simple terms is that the supply of goods and services constitutes a pie that has to be divided by a constantly growing number of people. When the pie is not growing as rapidly as the population it becomes relatively smaller and people as a whole do not improve their lot significantly, and that is what has happened. We will discuss the productivity problem in more detail when we look at the future of the system.

Investment versus Consumption

In a decentralized economy such as ours the consumption and investment decisions are made by the decision makers in households and firms. The market rate of interest after adjustment for expected inflation serves as a price to these decision makers and the allocation between consumption and investment is made.

One of the major concerns facing the country at this point is the question of the adequacy of the quantity and the quality of the capital stock. For some years there has been a significant debate as to whether the country is suffering from an insufficiency of capital. This issue has received increasing attention because of the relatively small growth in investment in constant dollars over a number of years. Further, there is concern because of the belief that much of the investment that has been made, in recent years in particular, has gone into capital to solve environmental problems and has not resulted in productivity increases.

As a result there has been a tremendous amount of political pressure to increase the tax benefits to the corporation. The belief is that changes increasing such elements as the investment tax credit will stimulate increased investment. This particular proposition has been hotly debated by economists for some time. There is no conclusive evidence to support the proposition that investment tax credits result in significant new investments nor to contradict the proposition.

If one steps back from this controversy and looks at the whole area in more of a total systems approach some clarification on the issue can be developed. It is certainly clear that no firm is going to make an investment unless there is an expectation that an adequate rate of return will result from the investment. Therefore, if sufficiently large rates of return cannot be found, all of the investment tax credits that one wishes can be enacted and investment will not be increased.

One of the major elements of course in determining the profitability of investments is the general condition of the economic system and more importantly, its expected condition. The businessman in general prefers certainty to uncertainty and conditions such as changing rates of inflation add to the uncertainty facing a firm. The decision to invest is made more difficult by the need to estimate the expected inflation rate and to speculate on the kinds of actions the government may take to curb inflation. The result is that the investment environment is made more uncertain and the effect is to discourage investment. Milton Friedman has described this effect well. "A burst of inflation produces strong pressure to counter it. Policy goes from one direction to the other, encouraging wide variation in the actual and anticipated rate of inflation. And, of course, in such an environment, no one has single-valued anticipation. Everyone recognizes that there is great uncertainty about what actual inflation will turn out to be over any specific future interval."[3]

Another factor of significance is the real interest rate. The real interest rate is significant not so much because of the cost of an individual investment,[4] but because higher real interest rates will tend to reduce the size of the automobile industry, the housing industry and, more generally, consumer durables as a whole. Therefore, with real interest rates increasing, the expectation is that the economy itself will be contracting and the environment for investment becomes less attractive.

Consumption and its counterpart, savings, are influenced to a great extent by similar factors in the economy. Savings because of the relationship to investment and ultimately to inflation and productivity is an important economic quantity. Savings as a percent of disposable income averaged from 1960 through 1976 about 6.45 percent per year. Since then the rate has been approximately 5.5 percent lower. In other words, we have seen an increase in the proportion of disposal personal income going to consumption in the last five years.

Of the factors that affect savings, certainly, inflation is a major one. The whole impact of inflation is to stimulate current consumption. The danger is that the money saved will deteriorate in value. Thus, the expectation of inflation will influence households to consume more and to save less. We clearly have suffered over the 1970s from that effect. Another element of significance is the effect inflation has on wealth. We have been experiencing a situation in which nonfinancial assets have increased in value. Thus, individuals owning homes or holding land have experienced a significant increase in their real wealth as a result of inflation. This increase in wealth makes the individual feel more secure about the future and tends to decrease the desire to save. A strong factor on the other side has been the increase in interest rates. The increased return that one can get from savings is a factor stimulating increased saving. The outlook for savings in the immediate future is that they will increase. The decrease in the income tax rates will increase disposable personal income and some portion of that increment is expected to be saved.

It is difficult to judge whether the economy has performed optimally in dividing resources between investment and consumption. We will examine in the next section the difficulties of the steel and the automobile industries. Clearly problems with investment are implicit in their difficulties. There is speculation, as we will discuss later, that our capital stock is obsolete. On balance, I believe that one must conclude, because of the distortions in resource allocation under the impact of inflation, there is a strong likelihood that we have consumed too much and invested too little. I would further add that there is evidence that the investment decision in many cases has not been wise and as a result the quality of the capital stock is not as high as it should be to compete successfully on an international basis. More specifically, we have lagged in investing in automation as I will discuss below.

Microeconomic Effects

Another phenomenon of the past twenty years has been the development of major weaknesses in several of our basic industries, particularly automobile and steel. Both automobile and steel are suffering from foreign competition. The competition from the Japanese has forced some significant rethinking by decision makers in the two industries. The belief of most of our citizens that foreign competitors can produce products that are equal or superior in quality at a lower cost is relatively new to America. Our history had led us to believe that no one was superior to us in manufacturing. We have seen our comparative advantage disappear, particularly in steel, and the need to protect our industries from foreign competitors is now seriously discussed.

The two industries are in my view suffering for different reasons. I would like to emphasize the problems of the steel industry because I think they are even more serious than those of the automobile industry.

The steel industry is affected differently by the Europeans and the Japanese. There is a consensus among steel executives that the American industry can produce more efficiently than the European steel industry, primarily because of greater productivity in American mills. However, the European steel industry has been able to make an impact on the American industry through the dumping process. Dumping in the steel industry is a natural concomitant of the high fixed costs prevailing in the industry. It is worthwhile for a producer to sell in a foreign market at prices that will just equal variable costs and gain the benefits of the increased scale of operation. This behavior is particularly profitable if a firm can sell in its own market at home at higher prices. Thus, dumping gives the firm the ability to lower the average cost because of the greater output.

A more interesting aspect of the dumping phenomenon is that a less efficient producer can compete successfully against a more efficient producer. If the less efficient producer is allowed to dump, he can drive out the more efficient producer. There is great vulnerability in the steel industry to dumping during a period when demand is weak in the American market. During a period of depressed demand the ability to dump will cause a significant deterioration in prices while total demand does not increase. Firms must match the lower prices in order to maintain their share of the market. Thus, prices will be driven down to the level of the price of the dumping firm.

This kind of behavior while destructive of profits in a downturn still might be something the industry could live with if it were able to make significant profits in those periods when the demand was high. In the United States, however, price controls—formal and informal—by the government have prevailed for over twenty years and have prevented the American steel industry from making significant profits—indeed, even profits equal to the average of all manufacturing industry. The result is an industry that has no floor to its price but has a definite ceiling. It is easy to see that such an industry is going to have difficulty in maintaining investment at a level that will continue to improve the quality of the facility. The expectation of profits is not there. Until there is a commitment that price ceilings of any kind will no longer prevail, the industry will have difficulty in getting the necessary investment made.

In addition to governmental intervention on the price side there has been governmental intervention in labor negotiations. The tendency in past labor disputes, before the experimental negotiating agreement was made, was for government to intervene and force a settlement that would generally favor labor. This history goes back as far as the Eisenhower administration. The net results has been a lack of vigor on the part of the industry to negotiate sharply and to be prepared for a strike if necessary to win its points. It was always certain that a threatened strike would be prevented by government and that governmental intervention would weaken the position of management with respect to labor in the final agreement. Further, it was recognized that strikes enabled foreign competitors to make inroads on the market. Thus, the experimental negotiating agreement was made and one effect of this agreement has been wage increases for labor that are greater than the increases in productivity.

When the steel industry was primarily a domestic industry with little importing from abroad, wage increases unrelated to productivity did not severely impact the industry. The excessive wage increases were merely passed on to consumers of steel in the form of higher prices. Beginning in the middle and late 1960s however, imports began to come into this country from Japan. As time progressed these imports became a significant part of the total market. International trade began to exert real pressure on the firms and called attention to the uneconomic behavior that prevailed in the wage area. The development of the Japanese industry in particular began to highlight the fact that investment in the steel industry had not progressed at the rate necessary to modernize plant and equipment.

There is general agreement in the industry that the Japanese are not dumping. The belief is that the Japanese through technological improvements and increased productivity can deliver steel to the United States at competitive prices. It should be pointed out, however, that this is possible in part because the Japanese steel companies in general do not earn profits of significance. The typical Japanese steel firm makes somewhere in the neighborhood of 2 percent of total investment. They are now attempting to reduce their capital investment, however. Thus, their prices are proportionately lower than U.S. prices. In addition, no one is exactly clear on the ways in which other efforts of the government ultimately result in the equivalent of a subsidy to the industry.

All of this leaves the steel industry in an unsettled condition. There is much uncertainty facing the individual firms and it is unlikely, therefore, that firms will make significant investments in the industry without a government policy that will make it possible for them, in the longer run, to attain an equilibrium position that offers adequate profit.

While I do not, for a variety of reasons, agree with a recent Brookings Institution study on steel,[5] I do believe there is evidence that the comparative advantage in steel is swinging to such countries as Korea, Taiwan and Brazil. The reasons are primarily new capital and low wage rates. There are no secrets in the technology of steel making and the most modern technology is purchasable. As a result developing countries with a large labor supply will have significantly lower wage costs than the United States and Japan. The result will be that a higher share of the world market will shift to those countries even in an industry whose capacity is already greater than the equilibrium capacity. In the past such threats have been handled by increased productivity in the American steel industry. Currently there are signs that both labor and management are recognizing the problems. It is not clear yet as to how successful the industry will be in overcoming its difficulties.

The automobile industry, also suffering from difficulties due primarily to Japanese imports, has a somewhat different problem. The oil crisis resulting from the Organization of Petroleum Exporting Countries' (OPEC) behavior suddenly converted the American consumer to small, gas-efficient automobiles. As a result Detroit was caught in a position where it was difficult to respond immediately. In addition, there is a productivity problem. The strength of the United Auto Workers (UAW) has enabled workers to gain wage increases that were above productivity increases, thus forcing the price of automobiles higher. Japanese workers in the automobile industry, in contrast, are highly productive and are paid less than American workers. The Japanese industry also emphasizes quality in its automobiles. Thus, the American consumer is able to find what he wants in size, gas-efficiency and reliability in a Japanese automobile. Further, the Japanese have moved rapidly to introduce robots into the production process, an area in which the American manufacturers lag. This introduction of robots has enabled further increased productivity and increased quality in automobiles.

Developments in both of these industries represent the kinds of changes that are happening to the economy, resulting in large part from a lack of capital investment in new technologies. As a result there is great pressure for some sort of protection for these industries. So far, at least, we have not moved in that direction. Nevertheless, as we face the future these kinds of industries and others must be part of a broad policy of economic development that must be examined.

It should be noted, however, that both the steel and automobile industries are in crisis in Western countries generally. There is evidence that there must be a shrinkage in world capacity in both industries. The problem for the United States and the world is to develop a framework whereby the most efficient units are retained, and the least efficient leave the industry. Government subsidies, dumping and protection will all work against an optimal world shrinkage policy. In addition, in the case of both industries, national defense considerations must be brought into the decision process.

Macroeconomic Effects

As we review the last twenty years it is clear we have been moving, from one economic nostrum to another. The 1960s began with a new economic philosophy.[6] The concept was essentially one of measuring the potential capacity of the economy and then using fiscal and monetary policies to stimulate the economy to reach that capacity. The "new economics" was based on an assumption of 4 percent unemployment as being the normal rate. The attempt was made to forecast the GNP on the assumption of 4 percent unemployment. This forecast was viewed as the measure of the potential of the economy. When the actual GNP was forecast as falling short of the potential, it was believed that the government could expand spending or, as an equivalent policy, cut taxes without the economy being in any danger of inflation. The theory was to work on aggregate demand to stimulate the economy. The approach, clearly, was a derivative of Keynesian theory and was embraced by the enthusiastic as a means of ending the terror of the business cycle forever. The theory was a popular and appealing one particularly because it enabled government to increase its expenditures with a feeling of righteousness, because after all, increasing economic activity was good. The concept of balancing the budget over the business cycle was abandoned and fiscal and monetary policy was joined together with the attainment of the goal of economic expansion as the motivating force. We had great success for a while, as the statistics demonstrate. The unemployment rate went from a high of 6.7 percent in 1961 to a low of 3.5 percent in 1969.

The "new economics" foundered on the difficulty of reducing aggregate demand once the system began to move and the economic actors began to expect increases. There was no way, in other words, of pulling back easily on the fiscal and monetary reins without causing significant amounts of unemployment. As a result the consumer price index which had shown only modest increases from 1960–1967 began to take off at a more rapid pace. The rate of change in the consumer prices, which is one imperfect measure of inflation, began to accelerate in the late 1960s and early 1970s. Finally, in August 1971 the government decided to switch policies and to try another method of modifying economic behavior, namely price controls.

Price controls became the answer to the problem of reducing unemployment while controlling inflation. The unemployment rate had started to increase as the government, with the cooperation of the Federal Reserve Board, began to allow interest rates to increase by following a policy of restricting the growth of the money supply in an effort to control inflation. Under the lid of price controls it was possible to expand the economy and reverse the trend in the unemployment rate while not showing an increase in the inflation rate. When price controls were finally eliminated, the inflation rate increased at a faster rate than had been true at any time since World War II.

While the economy was under price controls, it exhibited the distortions that occur in resource allocation when we abandon the price system. It was these distortions that ultimately forced the administration to give up price controls.

The move itself must be viewed as an extremely astute political move. With price controls, the administration was able to get an expansion. For example, if we look at either MI or M2 one finds a significant increase in the 1971 figures and the 1972 figures in comparison to the previous history and to some extent with the history after that period. The larger increases forced interest rates down and allowed the economy to expand. The move was one that enabled the government to combine low inflation rates with a falling unemployment rate. It is interesting to note that this is the only interlude in the 1970s when we were able to achieve both the goals of reduced unemployment and a falling rate of inflation. Since that time we have generally had a high or rising unemployment rate and a high or rising rate of inflation.

Since the latter part of 1979 we have embarked on still another method of control. This method is a modification of the traditional approach of stabilizing the interest rates. In essence the method allows a wide range within which the interest rates can fluctuate. Unfortunately, this method does not do an adequate job of controlling the money supply in a steady manner.

For example, the growth in the money stock (M1B) grew at a compound annual rate of 14.6 percent from January 1981 to April 1981 but at a −3.3 percent from April 1981 to July 1981.[7] Such swings create great uncertainties in the economy and make it difficult for firms and households to determine a smooth path of adjustment in the economic system.

The real problem with monetary restraint, which is our ultimate hope in controlling inflation, is the related effects during the transition period. At the moment we see the economy in recession, with the inflation rate going down significantly. At the same time we see that the recovery, at least in the short run, will depend upon the path of interest rates. With large government deficits and with the Federal Reserve Board no longer monetizing the debt, the government has to compete in the market for funds. The question is whether savings will be large enough to accommodate the government and private demand without driving interest rates back to the level where they will inhibit recovery. We see once again the conflict in policy between reducing unemployment and reducing inflation. The conflict exists, at least, in the short run. It should be possible to reach a position in the long run where the price level is stable and unemployment can be reduced. The question then will be one of reaching a low enough level of unemployment without having to stimulate the economy through an expansionary fiscal policy.

In addition to the problems of inflation and unemployment, the last two decades have also produced two other problems that are of significant concern for the future. One of these is the energy problem. We see now that we must be concerned about the supply and cost of energy. Since OPEC's first increase in 1973 the price of energy has increased significantly and has become a dampening factor in the performance of the economy. Energy is clearly a problem as we face the future. We have an energy dependent economy, and we must continue to find ways of making energy available at prices that will be consistent with an expansion of the economy.

It should not be assumed, however, that OPEC will exist forever. The history of cartels is one of limited lives. Unless the cartel is held together by the force of law or the fear of some external threat, the tendency is for it to break eventually. There are many indications that such a break will occur in OPEC.

Another inhibiting factor has been the increase in government regulations. The effect of these regulations in many cases has been to divert funds from investment activity that would have improved productivity to investments that help the firm meet regulations designed to achieve a noneconomic goal. My point is not that these regulations are necessarily bad, but rather that they have forced the firm to accept certain costs that had previously been borne by the society as a whole. The net result is that firms used funds in investments that did not result in increased productivity. The investments did add to the welfare of consumers and the regulations to some extent prevented firms from treating the air, the water, and the health of individuals as free goods.

Summary

In summing up our analysis it appears that the 1960–1980 period was generally a period of poor performance in the economy. The major reason was the poor performance in productivity. Although it is difficult to give precise causes for the poor productivity record, it appears to me that the major reason is the fall in capital investment. The period we have examined is a period in which many major industries fell under attack from foreign competition. It was a period in which it was generally believed that America lost the competitive edge in manufacturing that it had held for a long period. It was a period in which inflation damaged the economic system and our society suffered from both high unemployment and high inflation. The various governments over the years tried a number of different approaches to the system but none showed a long term prospect of succeeding. It was a period in which we suffered from increased government intervention in the system. As we look to the future it is the past period that has given us a clear delineation of the problems with which we must be concerned. The priority problems are the inflation-unemployment trade off, the reindustrialization of U.S. industry, and the basic role of government in the economy.

Prospective Look at the Economy

In order to gain a better understanding of the future it is important to look at the demographic data and its impact on the labor force. The data is a projection, rather than pure estimate, of the composition of the work force in the year 1990. In other words, the people are already born and the projections are made on the basis of actuarial expectations. There are several striking features about the labor force. The first one, as shown in Table 10, is that we will have a significant increase in the number of people in the

Table 10. Labor Force Projections (in Thousands)

Sex/Age		16–24	25–44	45–64	65+
MALES					
	1960	6,909	21,219	15,974	2,287
	1965	3,191	21,023	16,808	2,131
	1970	9,714	21,775	17,541	2,164
	1975	12,158	24,142	17,408	1,906
	1979	14,292	28,017	17,229	1,928
	1985	12,465	32,143	16,634	1,765
	1990	11,156	34,994	17,234	1,731
FEMALES					
	1960	4,635	9,343	8,264	907
	1965	5,877	10,049	9,299	976
	1970	8,115	11,935	10,684	1,056
	1975	10,108	14,949	10,909	1,033
	1979	11,604	19,342	11,440	1,145
	1985	11,934	25,686	11,282	1,044
	1990	11,225	29,883	12,100	1,043

Source: Pre-1980 data are from *Employment and Training Report of the President*, 1979.
Projections are from *Handbook for Labor Statistics*, December 1980.

labor force in the prime working age of 25–44. This group will increase from 42 percent of the labor force in 1975 to 54 percent by 1990. Correspondingly, there will be a decrease of the 16–24 age group from 24 percent of the labor force in 1975 to 18.2 percent in 1990. This change in the age composition should increase the quality of the labor force and should improve productivity.

The second element which is of extreme importance is the rate of increase in the labor force. As Tables 11 and 12 show, from 1970 to 1979 the labor force grew at a compound rate of 2.38 percent a year.[8] Such a high growth rate is significant because even with the economy creating new jobs at record

Table 11. Labor Force Projections

	1960	1970	1979	1990
Total Labor Force				
M	46,389	51,194	61,466	65,115
F	23,240	31,772	43,531	54,251
T	69,629	82,966	104,997	119,366

Source: Pre-1980 data are from *Employment and Training Report of the President*, 1979.

Projections are from *Handbook of Labor Statistics*, December 1980.

rates this growth in the labor force made it difficult to reduce the level of unemployment. In the period from 1979 to 1990, however, this growth is projected at a compound rate of 1.17 percent. (This rate assumes that women will continue to participate in the labor force in the same proportions or greater than in 1979). We will be increasing the labor force at less than half of the rate that existed from 1970 to 1979. This reduced rate of growth in the labor force means that even with a modest growth in the GNP we should have a significantly reduced problem with unemployment. In fact, the situation is more likely to be one in

Table 12. Rate of Increase in Labor Force

	1960–1970	1970–1979	1979–1990
Rate of Increase			
M	.99%	2.05%	.53%
F	3.18%	3.56%	2.02%
T	1.77%	2.38%	1.17%

Source: Pre-1980 data are from *Employment and Training Report of the President*, 1979.

Projections are from *Handbook for Labor Statistics*, December 1980.

which there will be a significant labor shortage in the economy.

When one speaks of a shortage in economics it must always be relative to supply and price. A price system will always allocate the supply of a commodity by price adjustments. A labor shortage means that at the prevailing wage rates, the demand for labor exceeds the supply. The result will be a higher price for labor to the point where demand is satisfied. We have had such situations in the past in prosperity phases. As the economic system moves out of a downward phase it will more quickly than in the past experience situations where labor is in short supply.

One effect of this situation may be an increased capacity of government to control inflation. As I think is evident, inflation has strong political causes as well as economic. In fact, it is probably accurate to say the political considerations have driven the economic variables. When control is exerted through a tight money supply, the resulting unemployment has always encouraged political pressure to change policies. With the relative reduction in the labor force the unemployment may be less and the resulting political pressure less. As a result we may be able to avoid the stop and go policies of the past.

In addition, there has been a recognition of the need to control spending. These two factors—the impending labor shortage, and the control of spending—can combine to give us a lower inflation rate in the future. As a result of this reasoning I do not believe that inflation or unemployment will be the two practical choices facing us over the next twenty years as they have been over the past.

Capital Structure

The far more significant problem lies in the need for reindustrializing the United States. The phrase reindustrializing, which I don't particularly like, has been used quite extensively. My meaning of it is that we must have a significant change in the amount and the quality of capital in our firms if we are to survive as a world economic power in the future.[9] We have seen that economists are unclear as to the cause of our decrease in productivity.

It is my view that a major effect will eventually be shown to stem from the capital we have in place. Inflation has a devastating effect on capital.[10] It produces falling after-tax real returns to capital when you take into account nonindexed depreciation. Clearly, such an effect has to impact adversely on investment decisions. In addition, the decline in savings has increased the emphasis on current consumption.

In the meantime there is a revolution in the type and quality of capital that is available and is already in place in Japan, the innovator in this revolution. The result is that capital is being made obsolete at a rapid pace. In some plants relatively new capital is already obsolete because the firms relied solely on American suppliers. Without an immediate increase in capital investment of the proper kind the United States will be in serious economic trouble over the next twenty years.

The quality of changes in capital involve, in particular, the introduction of robots into the production process in a widespread manner. Students of the robotics industry in Japan predict a forty percent annual compound growth rate to 1985 at which time the industry will have a value of approximately 200 billion dollars. By 1990 the value is predicted to be between 400 and 500 billion dollars.[11]

The robotics revolution is highly significant because it will mean a significant substitution of capital for labor. The capital will be of a type that will enable the economy to experience a significant increase in productivity. It will be a capital infusion that will alleviate the labor shortages that will be experienced.

The Japanese were stimulated to begin the robotics revolution in their own country because of the labor shortage they experienced. The Japanese had approximately three years of rapid population growth before birth control measures were taken. The United States, in contrast, had about sixteen years of rapid population increase. Thus, the labor shortage we will be experiencing in the 1980s is one that the Japanese began to experience in the late 1960s and early 1970s.

The Japanese moved to adopt "dumb" robots into their production process. These robots cannot see or think and do not have a sensitive capacity to feel. Nevertheless, the move to utilize such robots was a tremendously progressive step and has accounted, in my view, for a significant amount of the rapid increase in Japanese productivity.

The second reason the Japanese have been able to increase their productivity has been the result of their product reliability. The Japanese are able to turn out a much higher proportion of products meeting quality standards on the first run through the production line than American manufacturers. There is no question that American manufacturers can match the quality of the Japanese eventually. The difference is that the Japanese do it with far fewer hours of labor than the Americans. Part of the reason for the improved quality is again the use of robots. The other major factor is the understanding that it is far better to stop putting labor into a defective product than reworking it when it is completed. Thus, the Japanese workers are alerted to spotting defects and are capable of stopping the entire assembly line to eliminate or correct a defect while the product is in process.

Part of the reason for the contribution of the workers to quality has been the development of a new approach to labor management relations, a third reason for the success of Japan. This approach was again stimulated by labor shortages in the Japanese economy. Japanese managers discovered that they were having a tremendous turnover in labor, and management recognized that it was difficult to replace the people who were leaving.[12] In an effort to reverse this high labor turnover, Japanese management turned to the American psychologists who have been advocating participatory management for many years. Thus, quality circles were born and rapidly expanded throughout the Japanese economy. It is interesting to observe that the Japanese managers were much more sensitive to both the concepts of quality control and participatory management than American executives. Thus, ideas and concepts developed by American academics, for the most part, account for at least a part of the Japanese success.

I made a slight diversion to discuss briefly the Japanese economy because I think the expansion of robotics to the American economy and a change in the method of management are both critical for the long run survival of the economy. A second generation of robots is being developed in both countries. This generation will be one in which robots will be able to see, to think, and to sense more effectively than the present robots. Artificial intelligence, a field in which America has pioneered, is being applied to robots to make them into thinking units. As these robots are developed, American industry must adopt them quickly in order to maintain a position as the leading industrial power in the world.

A major source of difficulty for progress in the future lies in the adversary relationship that exists between management and labor. This adversary relationship has resulted at times in wage increases unrelated to increases in productivity, in practices that are antithetical to improvements in productivity, and in products that are inferior in quality. The concept of management and labor relations that now exists on both sides is marked by a divergent set of goals. Labor's goal is more money for less work and management's goal is to minimize labor cost per unit of product. To prosper in the 1980s we must bring about a closer conformation of goals based on the need to maintain the viability of the firm—the source of economic well being for both sides.

The solution to the problem will require leadership of the highest order from management and labor union officers. Labor must be made to understand that we can no longer tolerate wage rates that are not justified on the basis of productivity. Wage rates in the United States can be higher than those of our competitors only when justified by greater productivity. Wage rates that are higher than productivity justifies will result in an increased substitution of capital for labor and a greater increase of imports. There is no alternative, other than protective trade barriers, which rational analysis forces us to repudiate.

Management must take steps to change the labor-management environment. It must find ways of making labor a part of the decision-making process to increase the sensitivity of labor to the improvement of quality. As long as the United States was a somewhat closed economy for certain industries, the costs of its labor and management warfare were borne by the consumer. Now the substitution of foreign products places the entire cost on the producers. It was temporarily possible to have wage rates not justified on the basis of productivity. This situation, however, affected relative prices and demand and stimulated foreign competition.

Another area in which I foresee shifts because of the necessity of improving productivity is antitrust legislation. There is some evidence, particularly in the Japanese steel industry, that a larger scale of production can lead to a lower cost. Our economy has always been based on the concept of competition as the controlling mechanism. We have, therefore, tended to be careful about maintaining competition in the economy. Competition has generally been associated with the number of firms in a particular industry. Antitrust legislation has tended to oppose movements that will reduce the number of competitive firms. With the significant competition from foreign countries, there is a need to achieve a larger scale of production in some industries. I believe it is something that should be examined carefully, and I foresee the likelihood that change in the law will allow firms in the same industry to merge or form consortia when it can be shown that significant economies will result.

This movement took place in England and is, I think, an appropriate movement as long as international competition is allowed. It should not be possible for the firm to have it both ways, to allow mergers to reduce domestic competition and then have restrictions on the foreign competition.

Conclusion

I see the 1980s and 1990s as being years in which the American economy will again function in a strong fashion. I believe inflation will remain under control. I think that the investment that must be made, will be made, and we will again reassert our superiority in technology. The economy will prosper as a result. In order to achieve these results, it is clear that we must continue to develop an educated labor force. We need a labor force with the flexibility, for example, to shift to computer programming when manufacturing jobs disappear. We must be alert to opportunities for retraining labor in the areas where we do have shortages.

Nevertheless, it is critical to remember that there is an ebb and flow in the affairs of man, and it is clear that industrially the same kind of process prevails. In the 1950s, the Japanese believed that it was impossible for them ever to challenge the United States in the steel industry. In the 1970s the United States became worried that it could never challenge the Japanese in steel, automobile and several other industries. The reasons for the cycles are primarily in capital investment and technological changes. As we move forward and begin to invest new capital in our steel and automobile plants we again will achieve a measure of superiority. In order to attain these results, we must remember that in our economy resources are allocated by the price system and move on the basis of profit potential. When we freeze prices, formally or informally, for any significant length of time we begin to develop situations such as we have seen in the steel industry.

The energy situation will continue to be something that requires continued concern. We must have the research in the energy area that will enable us to develop renewable resources that can handle our energy problems. In the meantime, we must also continue to have the kind of investment in the search for oil and gas that is currently underway. I would favor an elimination of the windfall profits tax as soon as possible to stimulate further exploration. It is also clear that we must continue to do research to find methods for safely disposing of radioactive waste because our major hope in energy at this point still has to be in the nuclear field.

Despite my basic optimism, I believe our toughest problem will be with the humans in the system. We will have great difficulty in eliminating the adversary relationship between labor and management. There is no simple formula to do this, but I think every university in the country should be working to solve the problem. We need more places where management and labor can come together and be educated on the problems we face in regaining our momentum in productivity.

Of equal importance with any of the points mentioned is the need to modify our system of rewarding (and punishing) managers with the objective of developing more emphasis on long-run considerations rather than short-run profits. The importance placed on the annual statement by the market as well as directors for judging the performance of management and the firm has distorted decision making. The emphasis has tended to be on actions that concern short-run profits rather than on investing in research in technology that may have a long-run payoff. Strategic planning in American industry has been primarily market oriented. Strategic planning in Japan has tended to be on technology. The question of the method of production that will be used in 1990 is rarely considered in American industry. America produced the robot first among all nations in 1961. Japan did not produce a robot until 1969 and Russia about 1971. Yet today the United States is third in the production of robots, Russia second and the Japanese first. I do not believe this result is because our managers are inferior in intelligence to managers in the other two countries. I believe it is because of the short-run view of the firm that is taken by management. The major cause, I believe, is the reward system. In most executive compensation systems three years is viewed as the long run. We need a system that might tie compensation to a period ten or fifteen years in the future. Our Chief Executive Officers (CEOs) tend to hold office a short time and, because of that, also have less incentive to take the actions that will benefit the firm when they are gone.

In general I do not see the solutions for the next twenty years coming from government. Government must establish the stability in the economy that will enable our business executives to function effectively. Government must stay out of labor disputes and pricing decisions. It must control inflation and provide an environment in which rational investment decisions can be made. If this kind of behavior is followed, the adversary relation between business and government can also be eliminated.

The Japanese have shown us the advantages of cooperation among the major segments of an economy—government, business and labor. We must embrace this concept without eliminating our dependence on competition as a control device in our economy. If we can handle both cooperation and competition properly, we need have no fear for the position of the United States when we meet the year 2000. We have an economic system and a political system that work, and are basically sound. We must not hesitate to criticize and to make changes as they appear necessary. Neither must we, however, be prepared to change in the image of another system that may be working well at a particular point in time. We know what we need to do to be in a stronger position in the year 2000 and now we must do it.

I want to thank my colleagues, Professors Otto A. Davis and Allan Meltzer, for their many suggestions for improving an earlier draft. I also want to thank Charles Ritter for his help in collecting data and for his comments on the paper. Needless to say, I am responsible for any errors and weaknesses in the paper.

Notes

1. Knight, Frank A., *The Economic Organization*. (New York: Augustus M. Kelley, 1951).

2. Dennison, Edward F., *Accounting for Slower Economic Growth*, (Washington, D.C.: The Brookings Institute, 1979) p. 145.
3. Friedman, Milton, "Noble Lecture: Inflation and Unemployment." *Journal of Political Economy* 85 (June 1977), p. 466.
4. This point should, perhaps, be qualified somewhat. When the nominal interest rate reaches the 18 to 20 percent level and the real rates are increasing because of reduced inflation, they will have a negative effect on investment.
5. Crandall, Robert, *The U.S. Steel Industry in Recurrent Crisis*. (Washington, D.C.: The Brookings Institute, 1981).
6. Burns, Arthur F., *The Management of Prosperity*. (New York: Columbia University Press, 1966) pp. 57–59.
7. Federal Reserve Bank of St. Louis, *Monetary Trends*, (December 23 1981), p. 2.
8. Weber, Arnold, "Conflict and Compression: The Labor Market Environment in the 1980s." in Clark Kerr and Jerome M. Rosow (eds.), *Work in America: The Decade Ahead*. (New York: Van Nostrand Reinhold Co., 1979) pp. 268–280.
9. Simon, Herbert A., *The New Science of Management Decision*. Rev. ed. (Englewood Cliffs, New Jersey: Prentice Hall, Inc., 1977). This book was first published in 1960 and anticipated many of the developments in the use of computers that are encompassed within the term "robotics."
10. Fischer, Stanley, "Towards an Understanding of the Costs of Inflation: II." In Karl Brunner and Allan

Meltzer, (eds.), *Carnegie-Rochester Conference Series on Public Policy,* (15), pp. 5–41.
11. These facts are taken from a report by Paul Aron of Daiwa Securities America, Inc. It is located at One Liberty Plaza, New York, New York 10006.
12. Cole, Robert E., "Ambiguity and the Diffusion of Participatory Work Structures: The Cases of Japan, Sweden, and the United States." In Paul Goodman (ed.), *Change in Organizations.* (San Francisco: Jossey-Bass, Inc., 1982).

DISCUSSANT

Henry C. Lucas, Jr.
*Professor of Computer Applications and Information Systems,
Chairman, Department of Computer Application and
Information
New York University*

My own area of specialization is Information Processing. Several of the themes in President Cyert's talk have a significant impact on and in turn are impacted by information processing technology. In particular, I would like to offer a few thoughts on how the information processing sector of the economy has developed since 1960 and then explore its likely interrelationship with President Cyert's concerns about 1) capital investment, 2) productivity, 3) energy, and 4) cooperation among labor, management and government.

The Information Economy

President Cyert's paper presents statistics on the allocation of the Gross National Product and the percentage of the labor force in various sectors of the economy. Another way to describe the work force is by the nature of the tasks individuals perform. A study by Porat estimated that over 50 percent of the U.S. work force can be classified as information workers. (Though it is somewhat difficult to understand conceptually how a professional football player is included in this category!)

Information workers were assigned to two categories, primary and secondary. The primary information sector of the economy deals with a wide variety of services, for example, publishing and entertainment. I am most concerned with the secondary information processing economy which deals with the manipulation of data after it has been collected. Examples of secondary sector activities include most of the data processed by organizations to maintain financial records, production statistics and accounting records.

The Computer and Electronics Industry

There have been dramatic changes in the capital equipment available to process information over the last twenty to thirty years. Large scale computers today deliver over 1,500 times the performance of computers of 1952 and do so at a lower cost. There have been very steep learning curves in electronics and frequent advances in the technology which have been responsible for this kind of progress. The computing and electronics industries certainly will be high growth sectors over the next two decades.

Dramatic cost reductions have encouraged the proliferation of computerized devices for processing information and controlling industrial production. The current excitement over robotics that President Cyert discussed in his talk has been made possible by tremendous advances in computer technology. Because computer logic and hardware are so cheap, we are limited only by our imaginations in how to employ it in producing greater productivity. From the bulky vacuum tubes of the first generation of computers in 1950 to today's large and very large scale integration which produces over 400,000 transistors on a tiny silicon chip a little over 6 millimeters square, we have benefited from incredible increases in productivity.

In turn, these increases are allowing us to develop new products and services to enhance both the quality of life and the productivity of the economy. While I think only a few people may realize it today, the Moskowitz lecture in the year 2000 reflecting on the economy from 1980 to 2020 will look at this period as the "Information Processing Revolution," a revolution that will have impact even beyond the industrial revolution of the last century.

Productivity

President Cyert has already sketched some of the dramatic changes expected in manufacturing. The plant of the future will feature computer aided design, manufacturing and robots to improve productivity and quality. But what will improve productivity for the non-manufacturing sector? Electronic mail and filing systems, word processing, calendar, reminder systems and other computer tools will increase office productivity. New forms of communication will also help information workers improve their performance.

Doing some computations on President Cyert's data, one finds the 1979 level of capital investment for the farm worker at $69,420 and for the manufacturing worker at $13,206. However, think for a moment the average amount of capital behind the typical office worker. In most instances we are talking between $2,000 and $3,000: a telephone, a dictating machine, and possibly an electric typewriter.

Since such a large percentage of the work force is involved in working with information, one of the ways in which capital can support a dramatic improvement in productivity lies with information processing. It has been suggested that office work productivity has only improved at the level of 2 to 3 percent per year. An examination of the offices with which I am familiar leads me to suspect these numbers are highly optimistic and that we are actually losing ground! I believe that the electronic revolution that we are witnessing will have a tremendous impact on the productivity of information workers.

Energy

In addition to productivity and a need for capital investment, President Cyert mentioned energy as a continuing problem for the American economy. There are a number of ways in which information processing technology can assist in dealing with the energy problem. The first, of course, is through the direct application of computer processing to the problems of locating energy sources, for example, by analyzing geological data.

Business organizations now use computerized equipment to monitor their energy use and to control it. In the future personal computers in the home connected to appropriate sensors can accomplish the same function for the homeowner. Using either telephone lines or cable television wires, utilities will be able to control the residential energy load from a central office.

Information processing technology can be applied directly to locating and developing energy sources and to their efficient utilization. Another way, however, in which information processing technology will impact energy utilization is through the substitution of communications for travel. There currently exist a number of electronic systems for sending messages using computers and for the video conferencing and teleconferencing to reduce or eliminate the need for travel.

Several organizations are investing heavily in this technology for the express purpose of reducing travel. One firm has computed that it can save 20 percent of its $50 million annual travel costs through video conferencing. If total business travel were reduced 20 percent it would save roughly 50,000 barrels of jet fuel per day or 0.3 percent of U.S. petroleum demand at 1974 levels. Substituting 20 percent of all business travel by auto would save another 80,000 barrels per day.

On a more local basis, firms can reduce commuting by arranging for employees to work at home or at satellite offices using telecommunications to keep in touch with others. Some 27 percent of all mileage, 25 percent of all fuel consumption is devoted to commuting. If 50 percent of all office workers worked in or near their homes, the result would be a savings of 240,000 barrels of gasoline daily.

Cooperation

It is more difficult to find a role for technology in bringing about the kind of cooperation among labor, management, and government called for by President

Cyert. Certainly technology can be instrumental in facilitating communications among individuals. However, better techniques will not per se lead to more or better communications.

As President Cyert indicated, the responsibility will still fall on management to devise appropriate organizational structures and reward mechanisms. Management will also have to learn how to control information processing technology as it becomes an even more integral part of their business than today. The firms that succeed in the next two decades will employ technology creatively in new products, services and in their own operations.

There will also be massive changes in the labor force, both as technology is substituted for labor and as new skills are acquired by existing workers. Re-education will become an important determinate of whether or not we can achieve the full potential of the technology.

These responsibilities call for capable and knowledgeable managers. Our major task in business schools is to provide educated managers who can skillfully guide organizations into the next century. The comparative advantage of the business school is our ability to not only provide education in the technology, but to communicate an understanding of the implications of technology and how it should be managed.

Summary

Never before in history have we had a technology that offers the flexibility to design and operate organizations offered by modern information processing technology. The management challenge in the next two decades is to devise appropriate organizational structures and exercise leadership to see that the economy employs this technology productively. To achieve the potential that technology offers will require research both on technology and on organizations and a heavy investment in education for our work force. These factors must be combined with creativity and ingenuity to implement the changes required for the economy to continue to grow. Creativity and ingenuity are two commodities, however, that fortunately have always been abundant in the U.S. economy.

I would like to acknowledge the valuable comments and suggestions of Professor Margrethe Olson and Jon Turner on these remarks.

DISCUSSANT

William L. Silber
Professor of Economics and Finance
New York University

Predicting future developments is always a hazardous venture. There is the rather famous story told by an economic historian of a forecaster back in the 1870s whose job it was to project what it would be like one hundred years hence—in the 1970s. Using the existing transportation and production technology, the forecaster predicted that if the prevailing growth rate continued—then by 1970 all of the cities in the United States would be six feet deep in horse manure. Obviously, blind projections, without reference to pressures for economic and social change can easily lead to foolish prognostications. Fortunately, President Cyert has drawn upon his earlier incarnation as a first rate microeconomist, precisely to describe those pressures for change, while still providing us with a window to the future.

In preparing his outlook for the next twenty years, President Cyert has grounded his thoughts in a review of the recent past. This approach makes considerable sense, since evolutionary change is a continuous rather than discrete process. In his paper, he has documented the roles of (1) inflation, (2) the erosion of confidence in purely governmental solutions to our economic problems, and (3) foreign competition. But what is most emphasized both for the past and the future path of our economy is the lesson from the Japanese regarding labor and management cooperation. All of these forces helped shape the past twenty years and will help call the tune for the next generation.

One area of omission in President Cyert's remarks that I would like to focus on is the developments in finance that are related to the first two items: inflation and government policy limitations. I think that the role of the financial sector in improving economic welfare is often overlooked. Most of us use consumption per capita as the measure of our standard of living. As President Cyert mentions early in his paper, however, the *stability* of the economy is an important dimension as well. In particular, variability in consumption per capita over time is undesirable as long as people are risk averse; we prefer a smooth increase in consumption, as opposed to uncontrolled fluctuations.

Recognition of this objective was one of the main components of applied Keynesian economics: namely to smooth out the fluctuations in economic activity. And that is the first best solution—keep total production growing on an even keel. But during the past ten years we have learned the limitations of government's ability to stabilize overall economic activity. Some base level of economic fluctuation is inherent in the uncertainties associated with real investment decisions—less than perhaps we thought pre-Keynes, but more than we thought in the golden age of intervention: the 1960s.

The limitations of macroeconomics stabilization forces us to consider the individual's perspective—either as a consumer or as a firm. The question is as follows: How best to structure one's income and assets so that consumption over time is stabilized, or at least to provide the opportunity to stabilize consumption. This problem brings us to the use of a number of financial sector services, including: (1) well diversified portfolios to minimize the risk of individual investments; (2) secondary markets so that an individual can dispose of an asset at his own discretion in order to consume more when needed; (3) futures markets so that producers can hedge the risk exposure associated with price fluctuations. Note that in this case, some of the risks actually disappear completely—namely when symmetrical hedging requirements are uncovered by the marketplace.

Each of these financial sector services has developed considerably during the past twenty years. The invention of new futures markets and the development of secondary markets for established assets has been especially obvious during the inflation plagued 1970s. Moreover, the interest rate volatility associated with the new look in monetary policy since October 1979 has made these items even more important to those seeking protection from the inherent uncertainties of economic activity.

More specifically, the introduction of futures markets on such unconventional items as treasury securities, certificates of deposit and now even stock market indices, has added a measure of flexibility to portfolio decisions. The soon-to-be-developed options contracts on such instruments are likely to do even more. Academic economists talk about such developments as moving towards a system of complete markets. Practitioners simply benefit from the expanded financial menu.

Turning to the outlook over the next twenty years—these developments in financial services will no doubt expand considerably; but not because the uncertainties will increase. I quite agree with President Cyert's expectation that inflation will abate. But price and interest rate volatility won't go away. They are simply in the nature of the economic system. And as long as they are there, the stage is set for expanding financial services. The stimulus to further development over the next twenty years will come from the second factor that helps determine the quality of the financial product—and that is technology.

In his paper, President Cyert alluded to the potential importance of artificial intelligence to the production process. Well, the revolution in information storage, retrieval, and communication will have a still more dramatic effect on the financial industry. And the reason is not hard to understand: information is *the* product of the financial sector. Thus, the technology coming on board is likely to change the face of stock and commodities exchanges, banks and insurance companies, and even the venerable operations of our investment bankers.

Increased productivity in financial services will flow from the ability of many individuals to participate in market activities from unconventional locations—including the home, the golf course, and even the university. Knowledge will be easily accessible, capable of instantaneous updating and processing. And I am afraid I can only scratch the surface of what is possible because my imagination is limited.

The contribution of these financial developments to President Cyert's world will be in helping industry to control better the risks of real investment.

Entrepreneurs in the United States will have to undertake risky ventures in order to remain competitive. A more efficient financial sector will help allocate resources towards more effective uses. If entrepreneurs, in fact, can do their job more easily as a result, then the retrospective in the year 2000 might be quite a bit brighter than our current experience.